## Thank You:

*...my bride, Maria, because she's the one who pushed me, and enabled me to start the practice.*

*...my children, Jared and Emily, because I'm a better coach from having a precious relationship with my stepchildren.*

*...my own executive coaches, Charlie Clough and Marlys Hanson, who showed me boundary-driven authentic coaching and gave me a clear picture for what that experience is like.*

*...my entire book production team...from creative concept to copywriting to design to project management...thank you for guiding me through the sometimes long and confusing journey of publishing a book.*

*...my entire WOA team because they've been my mirror to push and cajole me, not only to complete this book, but also taking other steps that capture* The Connections Process. *Every person at every level of my organization added their own value.*

# TABLE OF CONTENTS

# FOREWORD

*Prior to starting my coaching practice, I spent twenty-five years in the project-delivery industry as a national and regional account manager for such companies as PSA/Dewberry, Bovis, and Gilbane Building Company. During this time, I noticed two interesting things: We, as service providers, struggled to convey our complex and subtle value propositions to owners; and owners struggled to identify impactful service providers. I learned that I could better connect with an owner, and consequently develop long-term account relationships, when I spent time researching and learning the important business and political issues driving needs for owners. When I did that, I was able to better connect solutions to the owner's challenges.*

*In 2005, I decided to launch Wayne O'Neill and Associates, an account development coaching practice focused on bridging the gap between the owner and service provider groups. We coach The Connection Process; our methodology that is designed to help businesses grow in a faster, more collaborative, and intelligent way. By showing leadership teams how to unhook from traditional (linear) sales techniques, and focus on systematically gathering intelligence and leveraging their value, we help them build the flywheels their companies need to achieve, long-term, sustainable growth and profitability.*

*Leadership teams need to learn their business battlefield and learn how to position themselves with clients and Project/Scope Delivery Partners (P/SDP). Success is about constantly learning, evolving, and figuring out the right ways to leverage what you know. ANYBODY can do this if they learn how to gather and assimilate information in a systematic and repeatable way.*

*I get tremendous personal satisfaction from watching clients master this skill, and develop into people who add even more value and impact to their relationships. Their confidence flourishes and they lead their companies to long-term, sustainable success.*

## Wayne O'Neill

*"Not only is Wayne great at account development, he has always been extremely generous about mentoring and leading others around him. When we started together years ago at Gilbane, Wayne would spend hours with me helping me improve my skills. He really helped me get to where I am in my career, and I know he's helped many others in this industry in the same way. Wayne really impacted me to the point that I now try to mentor and support others on my team in the same way."*

## MATT DANIEL

**SENIOR VICE PRESIDENT**
**GENERAL MANAGER OF TEXAS OPERATIONS FOR KBR BUILDING GROUP**

# THE STORY OF THE ILLUSTRATIONS

*When my team and I started talking about the design theme for this book, I very clearly knew what I DID NOT want. I did not want the traditional "sales executive" book with people in suits shaking hands, sitting around conference tables, looking at presentation screens. Those types of images absolutely do not align with my brand or my message.*

*The truth is, I'm known as an instigator. I like to push people. Always in a respectful and professional manner…but I continuously push them to think differently. I want to drive my service provider clients to be more creative about how they go to market, build connections, and develop sustainable and profitable accounts. And I want to drive the leadership levels of owners/customers to explore more diverse resources and truly leverage service providers…not just hire them.*

*So I got creative about how we approached the design of this book.*

*I hired an illustrator to create interesting and unique images for each chapter that represent the emotional journey our clients experience during a coaching engagement. The design process was a bit of a journey, and we experienced a few iterations before we finalized the 7 illustrations in this book. Ultimately, I'm pleased with how they symbolize the transformation in how people approach the challenge of connecting in the business world.*

*However, I do realize the illustrations could come across as "weird" to some people…well a lot of people. And I'm really ok with that. I want the illustrations to draw people in. I want you to wonder what they're all about. I hope that you read the description that goes along with each one. I hope they push the creative side of your brain.*

## Wayne O'Neill

**MAY 2014**

# RESET

## WHY YOU NEED TO STOP SELLING

The traditional sales process has always been very linear. Sales people have spent years developing and mastering sales systems to create control and predictability. But as decision-making and complexity of owner's issues has evolved, that once comfortable path is beginning to feel much more chaotic.

RESET

# RESET FOR IMPACT

This is not a "doing deals" transactional world anymore where just winning projects and securing scope guarantees the long-term growth and success of your firm. Instead, we have moved into a world where the ability to connect and articulate your value and impact reign supreme. If you are selling a complex product or service, you have to think long and hard about the process of reaching out to any potential customer. It's the starting of the conversation, cultivating of the conversation, and maintaining of the conversation that now leads to the more predictive building of accounts and, therefore, profitable revenue.

In our personal lives, we understand what it means to "click" with somebody. What's happening in the business world is that the process of "clicking" with your client is happening on a much grander scale than we can possibly imagine.

The "doing deals" transactional thinking is an insidious disease that's been culturally pervasive and reinforced with ingrained behavior. This is not a disease only infecting 50-60 year olds – there are a lot of 30-40 year olds who still think this way, too. The entire traditional growth model and process is broken, and it's one big co-dependent mess; most people just don't know it and/or refuse to believe it.

But you've sensed it, and you haven't been able to put your finger on what exactly changed and when. Worse, you're not even sure what you need to do about it.

*Simply put: You need to stop selling and start connecting.*

I have spent my career focusing on helping businesses grow through executive-level Account Development Coaching. I coach *The Connection Process*, a methodology I designed to help businesses grow in a faster, more collaborative, and intelligent way. By showing leadership teams how to systematically gather intelligence and leverage its value, I help companies build flywheels for long-term, sustainable growth.

*The most important and absolutely critical thing that I help service providers, owners and executives learn is how to consciously create authentic connection.*

Interestingly, I have found that the leaders with a track record of success benefit the most from my coaching. Often, they are more flexible in their thinking, practice some of these techniques intuitively, and are committed to continuous improvement. And it is just as likely that they've plateaued and can't figure out how to get to the next level. Until you reset your thinking, until you stop selling, until you understand *The Connection Process*, your business and your customers will suffer.

# SYMPTOMS IT'S TIME TO CHANGE

I've noticed that companies coming to me for coaching exhibit at least one (usually more) of the following six symptoms. If this is happening in your company, it may very well be time for a RESET:

## 1. PLENTY OF REVENUE, DWINDLING PROFIT

You're still winning a lot of work. But what's the win based on? Is it because you responded to a call for proposals? Did you win the job and the client says they "gave" it to you and that they're doing you a favor? If you're "winning" the RFPs based on price rather than impact or value, you're creating an even bigger problem. Clients don't care what you do or about you or your company. In reality, you are undercutting your own profit margins for the sake of false positioning and setting your teams up to fail.

Let me let you in on a not-so-secret secret: It is far easier (and more desirable) to compete on impact and value than it is on price. When you win work from a weak position – by lowering your price and, therefore, lowering your profits – you create a bigger problem than you even real-

RESET

ize. If you're connecting authentically with your clients, and providing impact and value, they're scared they're going to lose you (and your team). Think about that. It's a completely different negotiating process.

## IF YOU WIN RFPS ON PRICE RATHER THAN VALUE OR IMPACT...

*Don't sacrifice quality or value to come in as the lowest bidder. When you start offering value and impact, you start creating opportunities instead of merely responding to calls for bids. REFRAME value to solve the problem behind the problem.*

## 2. LEADERSHIP DRIVEN BY FEAR IS THE NORM

We are all competing in an on-demand world. It seems like we are constantly hurrying up and waiting. How often do you find yourself staring at the potential client list or project board daily, worrying over how you will get the next client or next job? You are probably even hounding your team and your client, trying to close the deal. Top leaders have a lot of things that keep them up at night, including planning for retirement and turning over a viable firm to the next generation. Another is finding ways to maintain profitability when competition is evolving and morphing on an annual basis. And, how do you really identify the new and evolving workforce to pull into your team because that's changing year-by-year.

What's really keeping you up is anxiety. And it's rooted in a lack of shared accountability in the leadership team around those things you are all worrying about.

## IF THE ANXIETY LEVEL ON THE MANAGEMENT TEAM IS HIGH...

*Start by taking a step back – both personally and professionally, and try to remember a time during your firm's growth when processes were less complex and more focused around the simplicity of the following:*

- *Are we keeping our clients delighted?*

- *Are we profitable?*

- *Are we having fun growing this business?*

- *Does our product/service connect with a client need?*

- *Are we experiencing "flow"?*


*When the answer to the questions above are "yes," it's likely you had sustainability and success. When we start to try to manage and control, we lose touch with what is driving sustainability and success.*

*RECEIVE the rewards of hitting the RESET button.*

## 3. YOU 'ROMANTICIZE' BEING ALONE AT THE TOP

Every leadership team both accepts – and has also fallen in love with – the romanticism of the "alone at the top" mentality. The insidiousness of this mentality is a much larger problem than you think. Business – and particularly the connection with your clients and your firm's partners – is a team sport. And it's a major blind spot when you over-romanticize your top leadership positions. If there's any one thing that causes relationships with your clients to unravel, particularly to your existing and target clients, it's the failure to build and maintain multiple levels of connection. Having connections with your clients involving multiple members of your team is essential to your personal, professional, and company's growth.

Owners are looking for true, impactful solutions to the big challenges they're facing. You're stronger when you can walk in the door with a solution to the true issues owners struggle with (A.K.A. the issue behind the issue).

If your business relationships are one-sided, or your network has vanished or is nonexistent, then take a closer look at your relationships, connections, and networks. If you are the "go-to" person for information on what's happening in the marketplace and your network does not return the favor of sharing good intelligence, then it is time to consider building better relationships with those P/SDP in your network. These are the partners you turn to, who you send work to, and who send work to you. If you don't have any or they're disappearing, you could be in

RESET

trouble and should probably start building new or repairing those relationships.

## *IF YOU FIND YOURSELF VERY ALONE...*

*One-legged tables are not very secure. A three-legged table made up of you, members of your company, and your strategic partners is a far better foundation from which to grow. REACQUAINT yourself with the people within your firm connected to your partners and clients to maintain that sustainable team.*

## 4. YOU RELY ON A FEW RAINMAKERS

In my experience, there's always a rainmaker – technical or non-technical – that Charming George at the end of the hall. You know who I'm talking about. Maybe it's been you all these years. Tell me, what would happen if your business development star were to leave? Ouch. It could happen. You've been around long enough to see it happen once or twice.

## *IF BUSINESS DEVELOPMENT IS FALLING ON A FEW STARS...*

*Develop a business development team that works collaboratively across senior leadership, marketing, and operations. And take a look at your sales Key Performance Indicators (KPIs). Are they based on the right criteria? In other words, are they purely focused on the top line? Or are there value components? REAQUAINT yourself with doing business as a team.*

## 5. 'THIS IS HOW WE'VE ALWAYS DONE IT'

You and large components of your team have been stuck: You think what you've been doing works. It doesn't. Challenge: When's the last time you worked with one of your clients at the executive level and asked them, "What's the impact of what we're doing at your organization?" Do you even know the answer to that? (Because if you don't, you need to figure that out.)

I've seen this metaphor used over and over again and it always seems apropos. It's the person you see banging their head on the elevator door over and over again. They think it's because they bang their head that the elevator door opened, but somebody else just pushed the button.

When a leadership team gets stuck, they're normally stuck on the logic of what they think is causing results – particularly when it comes to identifying and acquiring professionally satisfying clients. You think you're getting more clients because you're bidding more work, responding to more proposals, taking more clients to dinner. NONE of that is getting you more business. But until you step back and reframe, you're not going to be able to see that.

This is a big one. Just because you've always done things this way doesn't mean it will continue to work, or that it's even been working so far. You're fooling yourself if you think it will and that it does. Change, as they say, is inevitable. The harder question you're really facing at this exact moment is: Are you nimble enough in your thinking and in your business to adapt? You can't really afford not to change. You've never given in to fear before. Why start now?

## IF THE "HOW WE'VE ALWAYS DONE IT" MINDSET IS RAMPANT...

*Challenge yourself, your employees, your partners, and even your clients to innovate and start thinking creatively again. REFRAME how you do business.*

## 6. EMOTIONALLY HEALTHY PEOPLE ARE LEAVING THE TEAM

Emotionally healthy people like to work in places where there are boundaries, where there is a long-term respect for work-life balance, and where there is recognition that what you get paid and the impact of your work are equally important. As a Baby Boomer, I'm not advocating pure Millennial thinking. But the traditional mentality of working 14 hours per day and never taking a vacation is an illusion that's never worked. Today, people can practically smell when an organization is unhealthy, when you're looking at them as another warm body, and don't demonstrate that you both trust and value their impact. They realize that hasn't happened, isn't happening, and that it's not going to happen. When good leaders and up-and-comers start jumping ship, it usually signals deeper, underlying problems or conditions that could use some examination.

### IF EMOTIONALLY HEALTHY PEOPLE ARE LEAVING...

*They've lost confidence in leadership. This is not simply natural attrition. Don't fool yourself. Spend the time to figure out what's happening and why. Demonstrate that you value your team members and deserve their trust by engaging them with meaningful work, and rewarding them appropriately in both emotional and financial ways.*

*REFRAME and REACQUAINT yourself with your employees.*

The one theme that is common and underlies all of these symptoms is the lack of authentic connection – and that can only be addressed by you. You, and no one else, can and must decide to reset your thinking to work at developing authentic connections – internally and externally – and selectively decide with whom you're going to connect.

Throughout this book, I will be pointing out not only what to look out for, but what action steps to take to solve your problems – long-term, for the benefit of you, your employees, your partners and your clients.

I will address each of these symptoms so you can RESET how you think about these things, how to get to the root of the problem, and how to change business as usual into something long term, sustainable and profitable. You, your team, and your clients might even start actually looking forward to going to work again. Here is a taste of what you are going to learn in this book.

# THE GROWTH OF YOUR BUSINESS IS DEPENDENT ON RESETTING

Over the years, I have observed C-level executives within service-provider organizations struggling to convey their complex and subtle value propositions to owners (this can be the owners of companies as well as the figurative owners of problems that need solutions). And conversely, the owners struggle to identify valuable service providers who can help them solve their issues. While leaders may have been able to generate revenue despite that weakness in the past, this is no longer possible.

Companies on both sides of the equation are saturated with data, news, articles, information, opinions, features, benefits, case studies and more. As a result of all these people just trying to be noticed for any reason, there is an overwhelming amount of noise. Living in a multi-screen world with TV, bloggers, podcasts, social media and videos has only made it increasingly difficult to get noticed and be noticed...for the right reasons. Underline that – you want to be noticed for the right reasons.

All that noise, and the series of symptoms above, is a clear indication that it's time for a RESET.

# WHAT TO EXPECT

Everything I'm about to share with you is going to "feel" very uncomfortable at first. As a competent person you're going to fight it and you'll probably hate it. That's the nature of transformation. You wouldn't be the first to say so. That's because what I'm sharing with you will seem counterintuitive. As a competent person, you will fight it. You will hate it. I'm really asking you to trust the process. Like everything else you've excelled at in life, with practice, this will eventually become second nature. It's just going to be uncomfortable for a bit. Name one talented athlete who hasn't banged up against the "coach."

What I'm about to take you through is both strategic and tactical. No matter how strategic you are, you're going to have to understand the tactical steps to *The Connection Process* to feel comfortable. The following is the process and the way that I see it:

- In REASSESS, I'm going to set the stage, discuss where you might be today, and define some terms I'll be using throughout the book.

- REFORM will outline the seven common but deadly business sins I have seen committed over and over again. What's more, I'll provide clear, actionable steps you can take to start doing things differently.

- REFRAME is a deep dive into what you're probably doing now, the questions you've been asking, and how to change those questions – and whom you ask them of – to get better answers.

- In REACQUAINT, I'll show you how to take what you've learned in REFORM and REFRAME to build more productive relationships with your employees, partners, and clients.

- RECEIVE is all about what you can expect if you RESET your thinking, REFORM your ways, and REFRAME your questions.

- And finally, in RESPOND, I'll wrap it up with some tips on how to RESPOND to push back as well as how to connect with me.

# REASSESS

## IT ALL STARTS WITH A MINDSHIFT

This is your brain. The left side focuses on analytical/logical thoughts while the right side focuses on creative/emotional thoughts. Both service providers and decision makers must unleash the right side of the brain to authentically connect with one another and solve complex issues.

RESET

# EVEN THE MOST COMPETENT GET STUCK

With few exceptions, most executives I coach are incredibly competent at their discipline or profession. In fact, it is the very best and the brightest who come to me for help because they're the ones who, like you, are open to learning about better, more efficient and effective ways of creating a long-term, sustainable business. By the time I work with people, they are often beginning to realize they are stuck. Stuck in bad habits. Stuck in outdated behaviors. Stuck in dying methodologies. Stuck in a business that has plateaued, and perhaps even plummeted. More specifically, they are probably experiencing one of the symptoms mentioned in the previous section, RESET.

## *Leadership teams get stuck.*

As a business leader, you're dealing with markets that are far more dynamic and complicated than they've ever been. Decisions are just more complicated in this global, always-on market. The consequences of being stuck have become dire and diverse and have a negative impact on you, your employees and your stakeholders – all of whom are, more than ever, an integral part of the development of your product or service offering. It's actually shocking how few choose to truly acknowledge and address this.

So while it may not be your first rodeo, it's a whole new ballgame out there – and it's not the game you thought you were playing. Creating a successful and sustainable business is not just about solution selling, guerilla marketing, or even simply leveraging partnerships anymore. It's using all of those skills you've acquired much more effectively, deliberately, consciously, and systematically for better results based on authentically connecting. It's time to take inventory and reassess what you're doing, what you're doing right, what you need to improve on, and what you need to add to your skill set.

# FIND SOME RELIABLE MIRRORS

Think about how you learned to play any sport. Maybe you were self-taught or maybe your father or a friend showed you and offered you a few tips. You became more interested, but knew that casual input doesn't get you much more than an introduction.

Now, think about how you learned to do anything well. Maybe you got a coach who focused on lessons, specific skill development, drills, and maybe even videotaped you. It felt awkward but you continued to change small bad habits anyway. You got rid of your former habits and now you're playing with greater confidence and consistency. A great coach made you train harder than you would have to play, come game-time, so that you would be able to handle the intensity and stress of the game.

In my mind, that coach acted as a mirror for you. I don't mean that s/he mirrored or copied what you did. I mean he or she held up a mirror to you, and showed you exactly what you were doing wrong. Ultimately, that coach taught you how to fix it by showing you a better technique, and then made you drill that better technique so that those good habits became muscle memory. Malcolm Gladwell's[1] much touted "10,000 hours" to become an expert at something was not just about putting in the time. It is about practicing the right things and developing good habits.

Consider this book a mirror that provides specific coaching and describes better techniques that will help you develop good habits and an overall methodology for building authentic connections.

You can get the additional coaching you need when you seek out and employ other mirrors as well: people who have connection expertise, such as your P/SDP, clients, and service providers. When competent people can hold up mirrors to each other, share knowledge, skills and expertise, the results are even more powerful. They can see things about you and your company that you can't see. And they can give you feedback (by holding up a mirror) that essentially shows you what you need to do to improve. Don't err on the other side though – don't spend so much time practicing without testing your newly honed skills. And don't simply rely on your innate talent and never once look in a mirror. Make a decision to put in the time toward developing better, more effective skills.

You're going to feel like it's going too slowly as you develop these new habits. Once you've developed and practiced these techniques though, you will find that you'll go faster, almost effortlessly and perpetually.

# READY TO ROLL UP YOUR SLEEVES?

The challenges you and your organization are facing are complex, and the decisions you make about how to handle them have a widespread impact. How do you acquire profitable revenue faster? With dwindling resources, where are you going to find the funds for the capital expenditures you need to make? Who can help you? How you approach these very challenges changes your options. Slowing down a bit to learn and practice a new approach will open up better options for you.

It's no mistake you picked up this book. Something is tugging at you, signaling that you are not on a path to grow your firm. I just want you to consider this: It may be time to reassess and tweak your growth process. You see the signs that you're going to have to increase your profitable revenue. Fast. Projections are increasingly looking like pretty dreams of a better tomorrow. You're probably telling your people to get out there and beat the bushes, break out their contact lists, and set up tee times or happy hours with your top customers. But deep down, you know that it doesn't work that way any longer.

# THE KEY TO YOUR GROWTH MAY SURPRISE YOU

Let's anchor the discussion and define some terms. I'm going to be using a phrase throughout this book that is loaded with connotations both in and out of the business world. You'll be tempted to roll your eyes to something you may perceive as a cliché. Go ahead and get those eye rolls out of your system now and leave your prejudices behind, because this next sentence is important enough to put on its own.

> *The key to growth is **authentic connection**.*

I'm not talking about joining hands around the campfire and singing a heartfelt rendition of "Kumbaya" when I use the phrase "authentic connection." And it's not code for "closing." Authentic connection comes from empathy and engagement:

- **Empathy** means *actually caring* about the diversity of your client's challenges – as they see those challenges. Because that empathy leads to engagement.
- **Engagement** translates into crafting or facilitating solutions for those challenges.

What I want you to hear is that it may not be about you and your firm. It's about multiple firms that you are bringing together to solve your client's challenges.

# WHO ARE THE PLAYERS

While we're on the topic of defining terms, let's make sure you understand who I mean when I refer to each of the following:

## SERVICE PROVIDERS

These are organizations that traditionally provide services and/or product offerings. They struggle with articulating the complex and subtle value they offer. Often, they default to selling their specific service or product to fill a specific need as opposed to focusing on the impact of their service to a client. I help service providers understand their impact and provide paths to get that impact leveraged by their targeted clients.

## OWNERS / CUSTOMERS

It's best to see them at multiple levels starting with the C-suite, board members and stake-holders of a business or institution, along with the staff that operationally run those leadership teams or corporations. By nature, often these individuals are too close to their challenges to see them clearly. At the strategic level, they are navigating the tumultuous seas and seemingly con-flicting needs of the business, juggling capital expenditures and dwindling resources. The thing you need to know about owners and customers: Because they have a blind spot, they can be unsurprisingly incompetent at seeing their needs and asking for ways to creatively solve those needs. They have a blind spot because they are often too close to their challenges to see them clearly.

## PROJECT / SCOPE DELIVERY PARTNERS

These are firms that are already embedded within your target clients' organization and understand the decision-making process, as well as all the issues behind the issues that cause your target clients to not be able to compete as effectively as they could. They are pivotal in your authentic connection process and key to your coaching mirror to ensure the impact of your ser-vice is leveraged, not just hired.

They bring alternative perspectives, skills, and experience. Together, P/SDPs work on identifying and researching potential clients, their business and political issues, and the prob-lems behind the problem. They work to develop impactful solutions, and join forces to deliver and implement those solutions.

When you begin to connect as opposed to sell and seduce you'll find that interacting with your clients will become more rewarding and interesting than you can ever expect.

Let's go deeper.

"As a leader, you realize that regardless of the level of success you achieve, you can't stop evolving and growing. From time to time you have to make bold changes that will propel continued growth.

"When I took over my current role eight years ago, we had a lot of business lines where we were perceived as commodity-based providers doing churn-type-work. We realized that if we were ever going to grow and evolve, we had to change where we were positioned in the food chain. Because we were working through our partner channel and didn't have a direct relationship with the end customer, we didn't have control over the relationships, our message, our services or our fees. Somebody else was driving our services… and it wasn't the owner [the end customer]. We recognized it was time for us to connect directly with owners and create more meaningful and profitable engagements.

RESET

*"We took what felt like a huge business risk at the time and by-passed a group of our scope delivery partners who were, at the time, feeding us project work. Our fear was that those partners would see us going direct to owners as a threat and would find another partner in our service category to work with.*

*"What we actually found, was that by talking directly with owners, they were able understand how our services aligned with the solution to their business issues. The move didn't end up creating problems with our partner relationships in any way. Now all parties could show even greater value and impact when working together to solve owners' issues. So we no longer react to scope that is already planned."*

## STEVE CLARKE, PE

### MANAGING PRINCIPAL / OPERATIONS MANAGER
### GLOBAL BUILDINGS, JACOBS

# REFORM

## THE 7 DEADLY BUSINESS SINS
## YOU MAY BE COMMITTING

*There are also some subtle behavior patterns that have developed in the left side of your brain that must be reformed. So you have to work at improving some common "sins" that could be making it difficult for owners and service providers to authentically connect.*

RESET

# YOU MAY HAVE SINNED

There are seven common connection sins that I see my clients committing. These are common regardless of whether they're owners or service providers. It is entirely possible that the sins you're committing are hiding in plain sight because this is simply how you've always done things. So, let's consider some reform.

Though these sins may be subtle, they are in your way more than you realize. I bring these to your attention because people rarely consider these seven behaviors *sins*, much less problems. They are problems. I'll tell you why – and how to reform.

## SIN #1: IDENTIFYING AND SOLVING THE WRONG PROBLEM

Owners are overwhelmed by the challenges of competition and their own evolving marketplace. They send out Requests for Proposal (RFPs) to address each piece of their problems because it's safer and it's easier. And service providers who respond to RFPs containing complex services are trying to be professional and savvy.

It's a number's game.

Owners think: "If we send the RFP to enough companies who provide the service we are looking for, we will be able to compare apples to apples and get the best price for our needs."

Service Providers think: "If we respond to enough RFPs, a certain percentage will result in new business. So we have to find and respond to as many RFPs as we can."

The numbers game is seductive and comforting. It's the way business has "always" worked. We think it's predictable and (bonus!) we all get to look busy and productive. It has happened to all of us, including me. Overwhelmed by dwindling resources and the rigors of the operating model, we default to tactical responses in order to provide some immediate relief. We look for the easier, faster answers to the wrong questions, and address the wrong problems. We hunker down in our silos as if they were shelters, and we wait for the storm to pass.

As service providers, you may miss the real opportunity because you're too busy responding to the exact specs in the RFP. You're busy pushing your product or service instead of looking for the real problems, and the business drivers for those problems. As owners, you may miss opportunities because you're too busy putting out those same RFPs, and driving the procurement cycle for the "lowest bid."

## THE CONFINES OF THE RFP

Owners say that, once they narrow it down to the top five bids, any one of the providers can do the job. This "everybody is equal" RFP process gives an illusion of control and undermines the dire need to identify and solve the underlying problems. Winners in the RFP game often end up "winning" on price or a dynamic presentation, rather than value or impact.

Tell me: Do you think the iPhone was the result of an RFP? The more astute amongst you might pipe up and say that the iPhone was, in fact, the result of customer demand and that Apple was merely responding to the marketplace. I completely disagree, and I'll tell you why.

The iPhone was a solution to problems that the customer never before expressed. When it was first released, there was a collective "aha!" heard around the world followed by the sound of swiped credit cards. I want to also point out that the iPhone is a great example of how value and quality trumped a lower price point.

Let me be clear: I'm not challenging you to invent the iPhone. I challenge you to trust your instincts. Think about and really listen so that you can identify the issues behind the issues. There will be clues given all the time, though neither owners or service providers will be able to properly articulate or identify them on their own.

## SOLUTION: LOOK FOR THE PROBLEM BEHIND THE PROBLEM

At this point, I often hear something along the lines of, "Ok, smart guy. How do I really get my arms around this? Where does that start?" You need to let go of most traditional methodologies.

Clients do not hold you accountable to know everything. They do, however, give you credit for understanding what they're going through. So, how do you do you go about developing that understanding, that behavioral respect? Well for one, you can use the tools that you have at your disposal! Twitter, LinkedIn, and other social media platforms have made this far easier.

These tools can be used easily to great effect. I can't tell you how many leaders I see that have Twitter accounts that give you a ton of clues about what's top of mind and of great concern. Start following them and pay attention. That's part of the authenticity journey. You have to do it.

Don't forget that the customer is like a celebrity who is being accosted and "sold" all the time. They are accustomed to, and exceptionally good at, rebuffing and shielding themselves from the unsolicited and unwanted attention from throngs of admirers. They are even actively working against you as you attempt to authentically connect, because they cynically believe that most people have no idea, genuine interest, or clue of what they're really struggling with.

It's your job to discover the problem behind the problem and create "aha" moments – which starts with your willingness to look for it. That means research, or what I call *developing behavioral respect*. That's not something you get with a simple Google search. It means looking into all aspects of the client, the business, and the industry. How?

- Obsessively follow trends via blogs, news sites, and Twitter:
  - Identify 5-10 news sites and industry bloggers you should follow to keep up with the trends in your industry AND in your client's industries.
- Communicate your opinions.
- Listen to what other people are saying. Engage in conversations via your own (or your company) blog, LinkedIn, industry-related LinkedIn Groups, and Twitter.
- When you go to the once-per-year industry trade show, let people in your social media network know. Follow the etiquette and use the event hashtags in your Tweets

and LinkedIn posts. Search for other people using those hashtags. Follow them on Twitter and LinkedIn. Ask them to connect and tell them why you want to connect.

Put yourself in your clients' shoes. Observe their situations, their goals, their worries, what they do well, and where they need help. Hone your skills and stay abreast of their industries. Don't just listen to what they say they need – anticipate their needs. And as you build your knowledge about them and their needs, you will get better at this.

I assure you that staying current is easier once you have a solid base to work from, and when you work collaboratively. Initially, this takes a lot of work because you're not accustomed to doing it this way, but it will become second-nature with practice. Meaningful engagement starts here. I elaborate on how to find the problem behind the problem in REFRAME.

## PLAY THE PERCENTAGES DIFFERENTLY

You might be wondering why you'd go through all this trouble when you know that the RFP process has allowed you, more often than not, to hit your sales numbers for the quarter, and also identify some great service providers. What I'm proposing may sound like a total drain on your time and energy. Let me ask you this: Where are you spending your time and energy now to build connections? At industry happy hours, Friday morning networking groups, or maybe that big industry trade show once a year where you hope you were talking to the right people? Isn't that exhausting? And, more importantly, hasn't it become less effective?

Put another way, how exhausted are you working the numbers game? Most business development folks spend 75 percent of their time on the road, trying to get in front of 10 potential clients – and they make that one sale that helps them to meet their quota of selling products or services. Wouldn't it be great if you could still hit your numbers but focus your energy on two to three potential clients that you have hand-picked, working with project delivery partners to develop a well-considered, impactful solution that leads to a long-lasting relationship for everyone involved? And be able to do that without getting on planes every other day?

Stop playing the numbers game. Strategically select fewer targets by methodically gathering intelligence about both your clients and smart service providers. You're slowing down in this early stage so that when you connect, you can then develop things much faster. Come at this from five directions. It's not going to be instantaneous but connecting using this methodology is ultimately faster and more sustainable.

When you start developing behavioral respect, you have greater influence over the interaction, and it allows you to manage and use your time more effectively think of social media as a tool you can leverage to make the most of it.

Looking for and solving the problem behind the problem leads to the development of profitable relationships. It means that when you sit across the desk from your client, they sense that you actually understand their problems and are not simply selling them. It sets you up as a thought leader. It means being contacted for the value you bring to the table. It means setting your terms and not just responding to yet another RFP. Remember the iPhone: It was a solution to problems that the customer never expressed.

# SIN #2: NOT COLLABORATING

Internally, you could be dismissing or not even noticing people who could be pivotal to your business. Mainly, people who have knowledge about your clients and your industry. Don't dismiss the millennial because they "only" know a worker bee in the client organization. That worker bee can offer insights into a client's culture and business operations. Externally, you may not be effectively collaborating with your partner network, and you may only be collaborating with people like yourself instead of those entirely outside of your industry. You can learn a lot from smart people – even if they're outside of your industry. If you're clumsy at engaging internally, you're likely going to be bad at it externally.

What's more, we're just so busy in our silos. Everyone is on a need-to-know basis; it may not even be intentional. But because we're so focused on putting out our own fires, we miss being more effective and efficient by spending time collaborating.

There is no escaping the fact that you have to work at collaboration. It takes work to find and leverage diversity. But diversity in perspectives provides another key mirror to look at the industry, the client, and ourselves.

## SOLUTION: SHARE AND COLLABORATE

Have you ever noticed that, in shows like "Who wants to be a millionaire?" the audience is rarely wrong? It's why the shortest path to understanding your client is crowd-sourcing. Listen to the highly social as well as the shy, the young, the old, the marketing as well as technical and financial folks.

> *"It's as simple as this: When people don't unload their opinions or feel like they've been listened to, they won't really get on board."*
>
> **PATRICK LENCIONI**
> **THE FIVE DYSFUNCTIONS OF A TEAM: A LEADERSHIP FABLE**

On the other side of the crowd-sourcing coin is the fact that you will have to learn how to share information. I cannot over-state this: Sharing information is imperative. Your decision to share may not have an immediate life-and-death effect, but it does impact everyone you have a relationship with. Start sharing what you know, what you think, and what conclusions you've drawn. Share with your internal team. Share with your P/SDPs. Share with your clients, and let them return the favor. When you develop a culture of sharing, you begin operating from good, meaningful information, and you can all make better-informed decisions.

Some of the things people don't share (but should) are:

- Who their customers are

RESET

- What their evolving workforce is like?

- Who the stakeholders are

- What the operational model looks like

- Who their competitors are

- What their profit model looks like (the way profit is extracted, even a not-for-profit)

These are the components of business and political issues – the things happening inside companies and industries that effect their decisions (which is discussed more fully in RE-FRAME).

## BUT SHARE DISCRIMINATELY

After you gather all of this "intelligence" about business and political issues, be strategic about how you choose to use this information. You're not just dumping all of the information on everyone. You're being strategic about who you give the information to, why you are giving it to them, and how you're going to leverage that information to help the client solve their issues.

# SIN #3: FOCUSING TOO BROADLY

By nature, we get caught up in trying to keep more and more plates spinning. Both people and firms lack enough focus on the right activities. You are going to have to be ruthless at identifying and prioritizing everything from clients to issues to information dissemination to task ownership. You have limited time and energy. You need to make deliberate decisions about where you should spend your connection time, with whom, and how that should happen.

In 1956, George Miller[2] concluded that the average limit of the human working memory is seven chunks of information (plus or minus two), coining the term "the magical number seven." It turns out that this magical number, and pattern, has been observed and applied in numerous contexts including computing and, formation of elite military units, it is applicable here.

Seven to eight people make a perfect collaboration unit. And is about as many client opportunities as you and your P/SDP should be trying to manage for developing behavioral respect and maximum effectiveness.

## SOLUTION: RECALIBRATE, IDENTIFY, PRIORITIZE, AND EXORCISE TO CHANGE YOUR FOCUS

So, how are you going to sustainably put yourself in front of clients? Which clients? In which verticals and to do what? What can others do? You cannot create a compelling story if you're chasing too many verticals, too many clients, or doing everything yourself. Are you connected to ALL the right people (see more about this in REACQUAINT)? Do your service providers together have a complete solution?

The 80/20 maxim, otherwise known as the Pereto principle, applies: 80 percent of your results come from 20 percent of your efforts. Be brutally honest and strict about this. Identify what needs to be done, what the priority is, and determine which 20 percent you can realistically handle as a team, and what you can handle as individuals. Back-burner or cut the rest.

## DEVELOP AN ACCESSIBLE, WORKING SYSTEM

In both REFRAME and REACQUAINT, I go into great depth about some of the questions you should consider asking, the information to look for, and the partnerships that will help you add value. I also suggest that you develop a centralized, accessible place where you can share all this information.

A typical CRM will not work to analyze and evaluate all the client intelligence you're busy amassing. CRM is all about data. You think that if you have all the data and the reports that you can pull from it, you will be able to advance *The Connection Process*. But it doesn't provide you insight into whom your customers really are and what the real problem behind the problem is that you need to solve. It's like looking at resume to gain insight into what kind of person you're dealing with – Monday morning status meetings spent poring over spreadsheets won't either.

You can easily fool yourself into thinking that something is happening when it's not. You'll want a simple and well-organized dashboard that allows you to look at the most impactful of this data in intelligible, actionable, assignable, editable slices.

# SIN #4: MERELY SHOWING UP INSTEAD OF SOLVING

This is profoundly simple. Do you really think tradeshow booth #459 on the corner of dog-and-pony at your industry's mega conference is where smart clients will discover you? Be honest. Quit showing up in the wrong places. Don't be lost in the signal-to-noise ratio. Rather than simply standing there at the booth, what if you facilitated a meeting behind the scenes with a handful of leaders to discover what could be real solutions?

Smart clients are not at networking events or happy hours. You're certainly not going to find them on a mailing list that you purchased. Think about it: Are direct mail drops and anonymous, unsolicited email blasts all about you or are they about your client? (In fact, if the answer is "all about you" whenever you touch base with a client, stop what you're doing before starting that email, sending out a mailing, or even picking up the phone.)

*"…most marketers today [say] they generate leads and fill the top of their sales funnel, [through] trade shows, seminar series, email blasts to purchased lists, internal cold calling, outsourced telemarketing, and advertising. I call these methods 'outbound marketing' where a marketer pushes his message out far and wide hoping that it resonates with that needle in the haystack.*

*"I think outbound marketing techniques are getting less and less effective over time for two reasons. First, your average human today is inundated with over 2,000 outbound marketing interruptions per day and is figur-*

*ing out more and more creative ways to block them out, including caller ID, spam filtering, TiVo, and Sirius satellite radio.*

*"Second, the cost of coordination around learning about something new or shopping for something new using the internet (search engines, blogs, and social media) is now much lower than going to a seminar at the Marriott or flying to a trade show in Las Vegas."[3]*

BRIAN HALLIGAN
HUBSPOT

## SOLUTION: CREATIVELY ADVANCE THE SOLUTION

The clients you want to work with are out there looking for answers and smart service providers in unusual places, because smart clients are not doing business as usual. If you're doing it right, you'll be right there with them. Any other service providers that are following suit will probably end up being your P/SDP.

In today's age, this might not always be in a physical location. This might be in LinkedIn Groups, on Twitter, or in industry blogs. As in the real world, observe first before deciding to participate in discussions. Identify the disruptive thinkers, the thought leaders, and the thoughtful responders. Craft your message and your approach. Your name will bubble to the surface when you start demonstrating true understanding, asking better questions, and sharing what you know. Engage for interesting reasons. Connect through thought-provoking conversation. Be magnetic. Make it impossible for them not to want to know you.

Obviously, you can't throw out the baby with the bath water. This is not an either-or; it's an either-AND. So you're going to continue to create and respond to RFPs – and other traditional practices – as you develop these other skill-sets. Change doesn't happen overnight. But it won't happen at all if you only do what you've always done.

# SIN #5: GOING IN THE SAME DOORS

If, for example, you're a company that sells computer hardware, you're probably accustomed to getting into a client through the IT door. You like that door. Because that door makes sense to you. It's comfortable. You've probably noticed that once you're in, it hasn't been easy to get out of the pigeonhole that they've stuck you in. Pigeonholes are only comfortable for pigeons.

You are more than just the computers, laptop, and service agreement you sold them. You may very well be in your comfort zone talking to the IT Department, but since when did you need comforting? You need connections with people in other departments because those varied connections will lead to sustainable, renewable results.

## SOLUTION: GET OUT OF YOUR COMFORT ZONE

The way decisions are made in any organization is complex, diverse, and political. If you walk through a different door than usual and the person behind the desk asks, "Why are you talking to me," then you're doing it right. When you can answer that question with, "We understand that solving what appears to be a simple IT problem is part of a larger problem you're trying to solve," then you're doing it right. Your solution needs to solve the problems they have about improving their ability to engage employees or customers. Or it needs to improve their operational, financial or stakeholder model. This is not about going around decision-making protocol because there is no protocol for this.

The client (remember, the one who is actively working against you) will want to defer to their technical people in this example. Don't let them. It's a mistake. They don't have just a hiring problem. They have a leveraging problem, and they just don't know it. It's **your** job to influence, and help them understand how to leverage you and your project – and scope – delivery partners.

Just as all of these sins build on each other, so do the behaviors that you need to change. You have probably already started trying on these new behaviors for size. You're looking for un-

**WAYNE O'NEILL**

derlying problems and developing behavioral respect. You're identifying your audience and exorcising your demons. You're changing how you think and what you ask, depending on the audience. This next step builds on those behaviors, as well.

Think about how the questions (and answers) change when you walk into different offices at your client's site. What if you're walking in the CFO's office? What about when you walk through the CEOs door? Consider their roles and what results they are interested in.

In my experience, there are, in fact, *five paths of connection* into any company – two external to the client and three internal to the client. They are:

1. *Internal team members.* These are your team members who have a connection within the client organization.

2. *P/SDP.* These are your service provider team members outside of the client organization who augment your solution(s) and have a connection within the client organization.

3. *Navigators.* This is a person you're connected to within the client organization who can guide you through the organization and provide insight into organizational politics.

4. *Champions.* This is a person within the client organization with leadership-level influence who wants you to win for his/her own greater-good reasons.

5. *Decision makers.* This is a person with decision-making power within the client organization who can advance your goals and/or who writes the checks.

*"It's easy to fall into the trap as a consultant [service provider] of focusing on your own needs. You have revenue goals and quarterly numbers to meet. But to really find success, you need to position yourself on a team that's delivering on a greater goal of meeting your client's objectives.*

"By the same token, it's easy for an owner to choose to do projects the same way they've always done them…especially if those projects were successful in the past.

"While both behaviors are comfortable for both sides, they really are not the most productive. For example, a university who needs to construct a new campus facility may want to go back to the same construction plan they used on the last 2-3 successful buildings projects. But the risk is that they're making a decision in a vacuum and haven't adjusted for the evolving needs of students, professors, operations, and technology. Instead, owners should state their goals and objectives. And then work with a team of service providers who can help piece together solutions that help them reach their goals.

"Consultants, on the other hand, need to stop self-focusing on selling their products and services. They need to, instead, ask questions that help them learn the owner's specific goals. Maybe that university has energy savings goals, new technology that has to be integrated, a specific timeline to meet, etc. Consultants need to engage both internal and external partners who can bring value to the solutions. And consultants need to test their own relationship with owners and guide them to new solutions that can potentially help them reach their goals. In fact, I don't believe you're properly advising an owner if you haven't voiced your opinion and presented him or her with options and multiple ways they can reach their goals. If you don't want to just be a hammer out in the field pounding in nails, then be open, offer your expertise, and show the owner how your *suggestions connect back to helping them reach their goals.*

*"When both sides are open and transparent, the risks of being too narrowly focused are minimized, and the potential for helping owners reach their goals are maximized."*

**MARK COURVILLE**
**SENIOR MANAGER FORTUNE 50 COMPANY**

Presumably by now, you have spent time identifying the underlying issues your client is facing and how you and your project – and scope – delivery partners can help them solve those problems. Who needs your solutions? And who is the actual decision-maker?

Walking through the same door you've always walked through could be limiting you. Getting out of your comfort zone does not always put you in the danger zone.

*Let's pause right here. Are you exhausted? Maybe a little annoyed? No, I'm not clairvoyant. I just have a ton of experience working with leaders just like you. This is usually the point I hand them an elephant squeeze toy. They can wring that elephant's neck instead of mine.*

*It's reasonable to feel this way. This is a lot to take in all at once. Both to owners and service providers, it might seem like you're putting your career on the line. For what? Authentic connection? (You just rolled your eyes again, didn't you?) You have a reputation to uphold. You have a family to provide for and kids to send to college.*

*How about if we make a deal? Continue to answer those RFPs and have your Monday stand-up meetings with your sales team. But while you're doing that, start practicing this. Give it three to four months. See how it changes things for you.*

# SIN #6: CLOSING INSTEAD OF CARING

No one likes to be closed. No one likes to be sold. It just feels wrong. There's a reason you picked up this book. You already care. You're worried about what you can't see, that you must be missing or forgetting something because you are seeing the signs that your business is not growing in a sustainable way. You wouldn't be going to conferences, reading, or hounding your teams if you didn't care.

When you stop selling, when you stop closing, when you stop putting yourself in that situation – whether you're an owner or a service provider – you begin to see things differently. Have you heard of the Johns Hopkins Orange back in World War II? During the war, any sort of fruit was in short supply. Two different research departments at Johns Hopkins needed oranges, but there were only 2 trucks of oranges available. So it was clear that both departments would not get the oranges they needed to continue their research. Now had they talked to each other, they would have realized that one of them only needed the juice and that the other one only needed the rind. If only the orange grower stepped back far enough to see it, he could have walked in with the solution to each of their problems. That takes another level of caring, of paying enough attention, of developing that behavioral respect.

Clients need to stop living in their penthouse suites and start doing their homework. Service providers need to stop looking for RFPs and start doing their homework.

Neither side is practicing authentic connection behavior because they're so entrenched with how they've always done things. But when both sides RESET and stop selling (and stop asking to be sold), they start seeing better solutions to the bigger problems. Authentic connection starts here.

## SOLUTION: CARE AND SHOW IT

As one of the leaders of your organization (or perhaps THE leader), you're an integral part of the RESET. You're the driver. Who knows your business objectives better than you? Who sets the pace for organizational change? Who else can both see and make it possible to convert operational expenditure into capital expenditure? You can't delegate this.

As a service provider, you need to RESET in order to start creating work because you're offering value, quality and impact – not just a product or service. Stop pushing the close – that's all about you and not your client. Do not allow yourself to let your needs override that of your client's.

# SIN #7: MISTAKING THE PLATEAU FOR THE PINNACLE

There is no sitting back on your haunches or resting on your laurels. You don't do this just once. No one is going to peel your grapes for you. There are no plateaus in the growth process. This is about evolution. It takes constant recalibrating and a million course corrections. If you sit back for too long, you'll become invisible far faster than you know.

## SOLUTION: PACE YOURSELF

Remember, authentic connection comes from empathy and engagement – not from staying in an operational rut. Keep adapting your behaviors, and your bottom line will reap the benefit. But be sure to pace yourself. Be even-keeled. And keep feeding the flywheel.

*Flywheel: heavy wheel attached to a rotating shaft so as to smooth out delivery of power from a motor to a machine. The inertia of the flywheel opposes and moderates fluctuations in the speed of the engine and stores the excess energy for intermittent use.*[4]

**DEFINITION FROM ENCYCLOPEDIA BRITANNICA**

In the context of building authentic connections with clients, feeding the flywheel is about initiating relationships that will build momentum.

Once you put in the research, time and effort, energy doesn't get stored. It begins to mul-

RESET

tiply.

It's not always easy, but in order to be impactful and leave behind something that will resonate, you'll have to put the work in.

The good news is that once you get the flywheel reset and turning, it is easy to keep it turning, and it will continue to turn smoothly. Don't forget that you control the speed. Whether you're heading up that hill or coasting down it, keep your feet on the pedals, your hands on the steering wheel, and your eyes on the changing road ahead.

# REFRAME

## ASK DIFFERENT QUESTIONS, GET BETTER ANSWERS

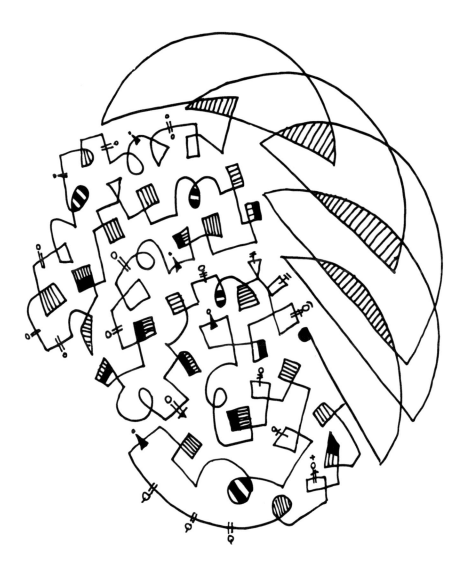

*Creativity REASSESSED…check. Subtle behaviors REFORMED…check. Now owners and service providers must REFRAME their interactions, which can feel disorganized at first. Though, in that clutter, there are new and healthy behavior patterns forming.*

RESET

# STOP SEDUCING YOUR CLIENTS: GET ENGAGED

Now that you understand the sins you may have been committing, let's reframe "doing business" so you no longer fall into those traps.

I know you're familiar with the traditional sales process – and by now you understand a little bit about why it's losing its value. On the one side, you say and do whatever you have to get the "big meeting" with potential clients. On the other, clients are accepting dinners, drinks, golf outings, and ego strokes. Both sides think it's working because service providers are getting time together with potential clients, and clients are being "schmoozed."

In the midst of drinks and business card exchanges though, have you ever thought to yourself, "What the hell am I doing here?" Well, what the hell *are* you doing there? Trying to spark a sustainable client relationship at a happy hour is like buying someone drinks at a dark and noisy club and expecting that person to become your future spouse.

Just being likable, knowing the right people, and knowing how they like to be entertained is not good enough. That's seduction behavior and you're playing the classic numbers game. Sure, you're pretty successful at the seduction game. You've pretty consistently hit your numbers. But, have you created long-term and sustainable business growth or are you going to have to go through the same motions next quarter to meet your quota? Is this the most effective use of your time and talent? You'll get a lot further by providing quality, impact, and true value.

Not sure that you're really a seducer? See if one of these statements sounds familiar:

*"I can just socialize my way into the organization. I'm a friend of your friends so, therefore, I am a good person and you should hire me. I'll take you to as many nice dinners as it takes to prove that."*

*"I know so-and-so, therefore I understand. Or, let me show you as many things as possible so you'll just pick something."*

Sounds superficial, doesn't it? What happens when that person you know leaves the organization? Did you just sell *him*? Or, did you actually prove your company's real business value to the organization itself?

Many of you might not equate yourself with being a seducer. You work hard to build relationships, which results in potential clients contacting you about your product or service, or you contacting them to check in. You talk about the Specific Problem and offer up Amazing Product A to handle their immediate need. You feel lucky when you get a chance to bundle it with a Monthly Service Plan – or better yet, super-size them to the Mega Service Plan. You close the deal. You hit your numbers. The client feels lucky because they know "A Guy." Everyone congratulates themselves on the wise decisions made. Mazeltov. Let's grab a drink some time.

What did the client really get? A Band-Aid on what THEY identified as their problem and no team to truly understand any underlying strategic problems. The service provider solves an isolated problem but likely misses the greater scope of work that relates to the over-arching strategy. This is not a partnership. This is not authentic connection. This is the game of seduction. Don't be a seducer. Seducers sell distraction, an illusion of power. There is nothing authentic about the seductive approach. Let go of seducing. The traditional selling and procurement processes are things that are done TO people, not WITH people. Do you want to be on the receiving end of being CLOSED? The difference between seduction and engagement starts and evolves differently.

If your client thinks like this (or you think like this when you are in a position to make a purchase for your business), it's a good bet seduction has happened:

*"We're getting an overwhelming amount of attention, so that guarantees we'll get a lower price and someone who will want to do right by us. Fifty proposals are better than five quality proposals. Volume will give me negotiating leverage and, ultimately, the best price."*

| SEDUCTION (traditional) | V. | ENGAGEMENT |
|---|---|---|

**OWNER**

| |
|---|
| • All short listed firms have a chance |
| • All responders can compete |
| • Negotiate on best value, but look at price |
| • Minimize interaction beyond technical interactions |
| • Timing of decisions is opaque |
| • Logic of decisions is vague to protect top leadership |
| [RFP Process] |

| |
|---|
| • Focused on finding solutions that may or may not be exclusively from your firm |
| • Looking for solutions/impact; not just looking for convenient, political selections |
| • Top leadership encourages open dialogue with service providers in advance of needs [transparency] |
| • Collaborative thinking around your business & political issues |

**SERVICE PROVIDER**

| |
|---|
| • "Relationships" reign supreme |
| • Enamored by the #'s game |
| • Obsessed with finding secret information that only your team knows |
| • Network obsessively but only with service providers in your "food chain" |
| • Decisions are driven by the fears that build during the last 60 days of a selection process - you may sacrifice your value just to win scope |

| |
|---|
| • Laser focus on finding smart clients who want to leverage your team |
| • Approach clients in diverse ways [multiple paths] |
| • Heavy emphasis on leveraging partners with services diverse to their own core offering |
| • Proactively seeking the business & political issues driving decisions in your target client vertical(s) |
| • Limiting target account pursuits to 5-10 clients with multiple scopes of work |

Your client may even believe that the more proposals they get, the more power they have. They may think they can wield that power to get a "good deal," without even considering they may not be bidding on the right business. If you were launched into space on a lunar mission, would you want a spaceship built by the lowest bidder?

If both you and the client believe that because you are giving each other the effusive attention you both crave (winning proposals, drinks, dinners, golf games), you're connecting – beware. You're not connecting; you're seducing.

What's worse is that the real problems are not being addressed. You know the ones I'm talking about. They're the ones that are keeping both you and your client up at night, such as:

## FOR A BUSINESS OWNER OR CLIENT:

- How can I find solutions that help me stay competitive, increase my profitability, and engage my evolving stakeholder?

- Does this person or business really understand my company and the industry I represent? And how would I know that?

## FOR A SERVICE PROVIDER:

- How do I get to the bottom of my client's challenges?

- Am I providing my client the right value and impact?

- Does the leadership team of my client really understand our value?

- Have I shown the client how to best leverage me, my company, and our partners?

You think you're getting away with it, but you're not. Numbers are seductive. Sales pyramids look like they work. The shotgun approach to reviewing proposals looks like it works. Procurement looks like it works when taking 100 firms and screening them down to 10, but none of these things will produce a sustainable business for you or a long-term solution for your client.

The old standard way of doing business – pounding the pavement to meet your numbers – will eventually become exhausting and unfulfilling. You can only do that for so long. When you authentically connect, not just seduce, you are not only doing business in a better and more sustainable way, you are also teaching your clients better ways of doing business. You must teach them that a handful of quality proposals will benefit them so much more than 50 mediocre ones. You must teach them that the best value doesn't always equate to the lowest price.

Genuinely sharing your ideas and values makes you less of a *slimy salesman* and more of a business partner to your clients. Remember, your clients' problems should be your problems, and making informed decisions depends on the sharing of information. Traditional and short-term thinking misses the point. Authentic connection is the key to the long term, the long game, and with the long game comes all of the power.

I love Michael Lewis' book *Moneyball* detailing the Oakland A's baseball team's unlikely rise to success. This is counterintuitive thinking in action. Before General Manager Billy Beane, baseball managers focused on the team batting average when they talked about scoring runs. After doing a proper statistical analysis, however, the A's front office recognized that a player's ability to get on base was a much better predictor of how many runs he would score. Because on-base percentage was underpriced in relation to other abilities, the A's looked for players with high on-base percentages, paid less attention to batting averages, and discounted their gut sense. This allowed the team to recruit winning players within their low budget. This changed the game of baseball. Before Beane, the A's team relied on the opinion of talent scouts, who assessed players primarily by their ability to run, throw, field, hit, and hit with power. Having been around the game all their lives, most scouts had developed an intuitive sense of a player's potential and of which statistics mattered most. But their measurements and intuition often failed to single out players who were effective but didn't look the role. It turns out that looks have little to do with the statistics that reliably predict performance. The A's change from buying players to buying runs led to a winning season.[5]

Over 90 percent of my clients don't think there's anything wrong with seduction columns, and they are amazed when the last two columns prove faster and more effective. If you're struggling with this, that's normal.

# FACE IT: YOU'RE NO CORPORATE CASANOVA

Stop kidding yourself. Seduction doesn't actually work. Nobody is really getting what he or she wants or needs. Stop selling. Stop chasing scope. Start thinking about creating impact for your clients. The small project to get you in the door doesn't have a sustainable growth plan, and being a great dinner guest doesn't make you a trusted collaborator.

The numbers game is traditional, short-term thinking that will give you traditional, short-term results and leave you with no power or control. Engagement and authentic connection gives you all the power and gives you back control for the long term.

For owners, the consequences of poor choices can become dire and diverse quickly, and have a negative impact on the individual, the institution, and the stakeholders. Your permanent record is following you more than ever before. Don't place it in the hands of someone offering an illusion of power. Everything that you are doing may not be as effective as it appears. Open your eyes. Be conscious of why you are choosing to work with a new client or a project/scope delivery partner. Focus on authentic connection rather than seduction. This applies to both smart service providers and smart clients.

## REFRAME THE QUESTIONS – AND HOW YOU ASK THEM

We've talked about the numbers game and how seduction is comfortable. Comfortable doesn't get you the results you need. And let's be honest here. The seduction game is actually exhausting. It's not smart nor efficient. You're spinning your wheels.

Sure, when we are selecting product and service providers for our own businesses, it's great to find providers we like to work with and be social with – and we understand when our own clients feel that way, too. But what we all really need in order to create a sustainable business is authentic collaborators who actually understand our problems, and how to help us navigate them.

*"Owners are marketed – to every day by people who are looking to sell them on an idealistic solution that will be the answer to all of their issues. For example, 3D models are currently a big trend in our industry. Rather than marketing to owners the ways we think they will be able to leverage 3D models, we chose to slow down and instead ask questions about what they want the 3D models to do for them. These questions spawned conversations about tracking assets, managing maintenance schedules, and other things that were driven by the owner... not us. These conversations helped inform us about their needs and where (and if) we could make an impact with our offering. The interactions also eliminated*

*the guesswork and allowed us to help them properly plan around their specific needs today and in the future.*

*"We are never trying to sell clients. We're having conversations in the spirit of doing what's best for the client and their needs. This approach elevates our company to a more strategic level and away from the typical sales/relationship building activities like golfing or going to ball games together. And I'm not saying that those types of social interactions aren't good. They just can't be the basis for building the relationship and showing your strategic value as a service provider.*

*"This process and approach has helped us fine-tune our thinking, and forced me personally to step back to really understand the people who are in the room, their personal risks and fears. And also focusing on relationships as opposed to transactions."*

**KURT YOUNG**
**PRINCIPAL AT WALTER P MOORE**

I also talked about stepping back from the list of questions you typically ask your clients about their problems. You have to get a broader view and observe the environment, your clients' systems and their behavior. This helps you gather evidence so you can identify the actual problems your client have, and how you can best help them.

I'm going to ask you a question that may seem a little crazy, here. But once you answer it, you'll wonder why you never considered it before.

*Have you considered that maybe your potential client doesn't really know what their real problems are? There is almost always "a problem behind the problem" that is really holding them back.*

*"I have experience on both the owner and service provider sides of the relationship. What I have learned is that for the service provider to be successful, they must be fully committed to their client's success. It is what Wayne refers to as having a 'True North.' Service providers must understand that instead of worrying about their own self-interests, they should focus on helping the owner. They have to trust that when they help an owner achieve success, they also will achieve success.*

*"Service providers need to research industry trends and current issues, understand the owner's goals, the issues keeping them up at night, and the politics impacting their organization. When they do this kind of preparation, service providers are in a position to stimulate creative ideas to help the owner solve the problems they face.*

*"Bottom line, as a service provider you can't just show up in the C Suite and talk about football and golf and then walk away thinking you had a successful meeting. Service providers must show the owner they are interested in helping them find success by demonstrating an understanding of the business and political issues the owner faces. The owner does not expect a perfect understanding of those issues, just a sense that you have done the work to try to understand them. That alone will form the basis of a stronger relationship."*

**TOM PAISLEY**
***FORMER SENIOR HEALTH SYSTEM EXECUTIVE***

# CHANGE YOUR QUESTIONS

Do you truly understand your client's problems? And do you think you know the problem behind the problem? What's going on "politically" within your client's organization? What about in their industry? What laws are being passed that will affect your client? How does all that relate to your client?

It's time to start thinking like a five-year-old. Ask "why?" again and again, digging deeper and deeper into the problem until you reach the problem behind it. Put down the clipboard. You're not checking off a list of standard questions, here. You're not taking a survey. You're trying to understand.

Don't ask the person or organization you are studying. Ask people who have worked with them. Ask their partners. Ask people in other departments. I will go further into the practice of tapping into untapped individuals in the next section, but the idea here is to reach out to people around your subject for perspective on the subject. The person you're trying to study has no perspective on themselves.

Armed with a *Client Whisperer mentality* that looks at the whole picture, and digging deeper by asking "why?" as many times as it takes to understand the problem behind the problem, you are making large strides toward authentic connection. But worse, you're leaving professionally satisfying relationships and impact on the table.

Both sides are accountable for connection. Service providers ask owners diagnostic questions, but these will only get both sides so far. They will not solve the problem behind the problem. They will only address symptoms of much larger and more strategic issues. On both sides, the "why" questions need to outnumber the "what" questions three-to-one. You are no longer trying to seduce your clients into doing business with you.

## OWNERS:

- Why are our customers not engaging us in the same way?

- Why have our operational models evolved under our feet?

- Why have stakeholders become more demanding of the impact that we provide, and expect greater social responsibility?

- Why is it so much more difficult to extract profit from the unique offerings we have put together?

## SERVICE PROVIDERS:

- Why do you perceive the scope we're discussing will help solve your issues of employee engagement, customer retention, and more effective operating models?

- Why are you so committed to the way you want to leverage those services to be effective?

# ADOPT A CSI APPROACH

Discovering and solving the problem behind the problem is a CSI-like process. In crime scene investigation, a diverse team of experts ask their questions and apply their diverse skills and perspective to solve the crime. This is the same methodology a smart service provider uses to decipher the client's problem behind the problem, and ultimately propose a solution

People don't explain things sequentially. You need a left-brain tool that's not just data-driven like traditional CRM software. It must also help you look for patterns and connections. You're an investigator. Your job is to pin the information to the board and look at it collectively with your team and the client to decipher the problem. Deciphering is a fundamental component of showing respect, and building connection with your client.

When you change the questions, you'll notice it's easier to see that you need to look elsewhere to find better answers. You start looking for the answers in the same places your smart clients are looking for them. Smart clients stay on top of what's edgy inside their market. They attend events full of forward-thinking people outside of their market. They follow non-linear thinkers and welcome a diverse array of disruptive solutions. They seek knowledge, wisdom and insight instead of contacts.

You'll see that when you start looking for answers in the same places your clients are, you gain two important things:

1. Valuable insight about your client, their industry, and the problems they are actually trying to solve.

2. Visibility to the other smart service providers who are looking for the same answers you are. These other providers are great candidates for allies and P/SDPs who can help you gather the intelligence you both need to deliver a genuine and comprehensive solution to the client.

*"Using a system to monitor your business development progress is not about data entry. That's the problem with most CRM systems. The higher-ups look at the weekly CRM reports and think… this sales rep is doing great! He met with four people this week and made 15 phone calls on projects in the pipeline. The problem is that there's no depth to the activity information. Like, what level of influence does the person they met with or called have? Will any of their activities this week truly drive us closer to an engagement? Most CRMs are designed and viewed by management as a way to track activity and are really not leveraged to measure true progress on active revenue pursuits.*

*"An effective system should ask harder questions up-front that force you to think through the reasons why you are pursuing a project. Those questions should cause the team to be more strategic about how they choose to spend their time and also which projects they will choose to pursue.*

*The system should also be actively managed, revisited and tweaked as the whole team learns more about the opportunity, the project influencers, internal champions, decision-makers, project delivery partners, and business and political issues.*

## Client Intelligence / Capture Planning

### Target Account

🌐 **ABC COMPANY**
Founded: 1983
Private
Annual Rev: $50 M (est.)

**INDUSTRIES/VERTICALS**
Higher Education
Healthcare
Governtment/ Federal/ State/ Local

**MAIN OFFERINGS**
Offering A
Offering B

### Project/Scope

**DELIVERY PARTNERS**
XYZ Software Company
Insight Consulting Firm
All Brand Equipment Provider
Worldwide Engineering Firm

### Differentiators

Can bring diverse firms together for comprehensive solution

Can extract op-ex savings to maximize cap-ex spend

Can address underlying client silo issues

### Business & Political Issues

Non-Collaborative Culture
Increasing Regional Competition
Increasing Pressure by Diverse Stakeholders
Need 20 percent growth

### Positioning Tactics

Blitz Meeting with several key service providers

Meeting with Insight Consulting Firm

Discussion with three recently departed executives from Target Company

Gain political insight from Executive Placement Firm w/ experience in this vertical

RESET

*"This will take hard work from the entire team, but will minimize the amount of time spent doing data entry. And most importantly, it will minimize time spent in places that aren't likely to lead to profitable revenue. When done right, your leadership team is left with lessons learned about the types of projects that were worth pursuing and those that were not."*

**RYAN SCHWAB**
**VICE PRESIDENT NETWORK SERVICES, WALKER ENGINEERING**

# GET CREATIVE

You're all about the numbers, the bottom line. You've left-brained it this far. Creativity is something that other people do. If you've been creative, it's something that hit like a thunderbolt in the middle of the night jolting you into action. Right?

Here's a little something to ponder: most of the time creative ideas emerge out of a repeatable process. David Kelley, founder of the design firm Ideo and the Stanford d.school, believes creativity stems from divergent thinking, utilizes both sides of the brain, and results in analytical solutions that solve every problem and guide every decision. According to Kelley's article entitled "Design Thinking," the creative process involves, in order:

1. Understanding

2. Observation

3. Brainstorming

4. Prototyping

Most people want to skip steps 1 and 2, understanding and observation, and jump directly to step 3: brainstorming. If you skip the first two steps, you miss the true value of the process. Most innovative ideas usually come from learning to listen with emotional intelligence in order to fully understand the issues and observe what is of true value to your clients. Only then can you begin to think and act strategically.

Take the time to:

- *Identify the problem*
- *Understand the business and political issues behind the problem*
- *Gather client and emotional intelligence through observation and insights from diverse people in various departments who work closely with your clients and know their needs*
- *Break apart the problem before you put it back together in a whole new way*

It is in that last step, the synthesis step, that the creative leap occurs. Don't jump to judgment too quickly. Come at the problem sideways. When you're trying to connect with a client, use the diversity of demographics, different viewpoints, to receive a diversity of answers to the why questions.

*"Most service providers don't take the time to understand a company's business and political issues. Speaking as somebody with leadership experience on both the service provider and owner sides of the equation, I have seen first-hand the value in slowing things down and really committing to identifying the special circumstances – both internal and external – that ultimately drive client decisions.*

*"In my current role [on the owner side], I recently worked with a service provider who actually showed that they care about what's going on in our organization, and showed interest in understanding our issues. As a result, I was willing to spend time helping them navigate through various*

RESET

*parts of our organization. I didn't do this because I liked them. I did this because I recognized they were listening to and responding to our specific needs. They didn't come to us with a product they wanted to sell us because that's what they offer. They put together a solution that was specifically based on what we needed. And they delivered metrics that tracked against our business goals, which built a great deal of credibility with our organization. Their level of commitment and dedication to understanding our business and political issues ultimately built trust and will make them a valuable long-term partner to our organization."*

**ANDY DRAPER**
**CHIEF INFORMATION OFFICER AT HCA GULF COAST DIVISION**

This is not easy. This involves structuring diverse opinions in a group and then following a creative process that doesn't leave out the first two (and most important) steps of understanding and observing before jumping to brainstorming.

The way this impacts the client connection process is that many times, certain people – those who are technical, younger, or who touch clients in a different way – are not assessed for their opinion on how to connect with the clients. I don't believe this is a sin, but more a lack of recognition that those individuals have insights that allow the company to connect in a much more authentic manner.

Think about it. If you tap into these typically untapped individuals, if you gather their thoughts and opinions, you are getting truly unique insights into the real problems your client is facing. Not only that, but you are also creating a much more authentic relationship with your client because you have the whole picture.

And that last step – leading you to a creative leap, breaking apart the problem to put it together in a whole new way – becomes much easier when you have diverse insights from various individuals.

If you take a single problem and apply the insights from multiple individuals, you can break apart that problem into various angles and even various steps. Suddenly you have a bird's eye view of a problem the client may not even know they had, and you are in a prime position to solve it.

As a business leader, you must reframe the questions for your own business, as well. Your resources, environment, and systems include IT, facilities, and both internal and external P/SDP that make up your team. Ask the hard questions of them and of yourself. You can no longer afford to continue to do business as usual.

# NOW YOU HAVE A CHANCE TO PROVIDE IMPACT

When you start seeing and embracing the problem behind the problem, you have a much stronger chance to provide impact instead of just responding to their need. You become valuable. The client stops asking about scope and hours and procurement diligence when they see that you start to grasp the problems behind the problems and make recommendations that deliver value and impact. They start asking you for your opinions, your experience – your brain. The painful procurement cycle that we loathe becomes irrelevant.

When you are in the client position in your own business, start looking for those smart service providers who add real value and whose ideas, partners, and solutions have actual impact. You'll sleep better. And you'll lead by example for your own clients.

*"When trying to connect at higher levels of an organization, you can't underestimate the importance of communicating your impact and value. The natural tendency – especially for companies that sell software, or anything technically based – is to focus the conversation on features and functionality. I have found that when you slow down and take the time as a team to develop a narrative around your product's impact, it actu-*

*ally speeds up the process of connecting with decision makers. What they [decision makers] ultimately care about is finding solutions that help them reach their business and organizational goals. That being said, it's important to have features and functionality that can deliver the type of impact customers are looking for.*

*"Our development team created a robust platform that includes all of the features users are seeking. But what we emphasize with decision makers is our 'Stewardship to Equity' strategy. By properly managing their assets – using our platform – organizations can free up large sums of cash that they can use to fund capital projects. That message resonates with leadership because they struggle with finding funding sources for projects that bring growth and sustainability to their organizations."*

**DAVE MOSBY**
**SENIOR CONSULTANT, ASSETWORKS**

# ENGAGEMENT CAN BE CLUMSY

Take a breather here. Engagement is clumsier than normal box-checking selling. Getting competent owners to leverage you is not a straight-line process. Finding service providers who are truly willing to embrace your problem behind problem and leveraging a CSI strategy to find solutions instead of pre-packaged services is clumsy. But engagement can be so much more rewarding than the procurement/sales cycle you've come to expect.

This is about the time I hear exasperated, frustrated leaders ask, "If this way of doing business is so brilliant, why aren't more people doing it this way?" The answer is, because:

- Some people don't know that authentic connection is a way to do business

- People are not used to doing it this way and don't know how

- What they used to do worked once or worked well enough

- This way feels like it will take too long because it is complex

Service providers are accustomed to selling their specific product or service instead of looking for true solutions to their clients' problems. Clients are accustomed to thinking of their problems in their disparate silos. Both owners and service providers accept a linear view of the engagement process. They all think that I'm talking about procurement and they all agree that procurement is a 12-18 month process. Not only is everyone unaccustomed and inexperienced at stepping back and looking at their problems holistically, sometimes it's impossible to see problems without someone else pointing them out.

We're no longer talking procurement. We're talking about engagement. Connection. Impact. And rules get bent for impact. You have to be able to articulate the impact you can bring to an organization. Until you do, the rules will never change for you.

It's like the process of improving a golf swing. It's easy to tell that you're not getting the result you want and that you're doing something wrong – but it's very hard to know what exactly to correct. You can't see your own swing. It helps to work with someone (even multiple people with diverse points of view) with an outside frame of reference who can point out the weaknesses you overlook or simply can't see. Not only does it take that outside perspective, it takes practice. How much practice? As much as you need and for however long it takes.

Connection is a team sport. Winning teams don't merely practice, they "practice perfect," to steal Lemov's[7] phrase from *Practice Perfect: 42 Rules for Getting Better at Getting Better*[5]. That is, winning teams practice efficiently, with humility and focus. They practice right actions until they become habit. They admit that they don't know everything and declare they can do better. They focus on higher-level work.

Authentic connection, true engagement, thinking about the problems behind the problems, staying current, and asking better questions are game-changing behaviors and take both time and practice. It's probably going to feel clumsy and awkward at first for most of you. For some of you, you may only be missing a few pieces of the puzzle.

And it will require LOTS of teamwork.

# REACQUAINT

## A NEW PERSPECTIVE
## ON YOUR RELATIONSHIPS

*Your strategic thinking around building authentic connections sits at the middle of every-*

*thing. Now owners and service providers must think about their overall approach. How are*

*they assessing and capitalizing on all of the companies, partners and resources around them?*

RESET

# EVEN 007 HAS
# A SUPPORT TEAM

Reacquaint yourself with P/SDPs who can help you grow your business. You need to build your leverage team. You are not a rock, nor are you an island. You can't – and shouldn't – do this alone. You need a diverse and reliable set of project delivery partners, both internally and externally. These partners will not only help you to gather, record, and analyze this intelligence, but they will help you to both identify and solve the problems.

In order to build that sought – after authentic connection with a smart client, you need to rely on no more than 10 smart P/SDPs who would each focus on their areas of expertise. Most firms have only a couple. Remember, you are an investigator and the problem behind the problem cannot be deciphered without a diverse team considering all patterns, angles, and connections. That is too much weight for two partners.

The most effective P/SDPs are the ones who – right after they think about themselves – think about you. Look for people outside of your food chain who possess client intelligence rooted in EQ, who will understand the language of the client, and they will appreciate your interest in their input.

It is easier to acquire client intelligence from P/SDPs outside the food chain because they are not your direct competition. In fact, you are empowering them with the opportunity to contribute. As for those inside your food chain, they need to see that you are both trying to understand the same customer and not necessarily bring them work. This too is not about seduction. The goal isn't to trade favors. The goal is to understand the client and earn their respect – and that respect is hard-won. There is no way around it.

*"A traditional (more linear) approach makes people feel comfortable because it's what they already know. But just because a process is comfortable doesn't mean it's effective. Developing business as part of a col-*

*WAYNE O'NEILL*

laborative team is hard work and requires you to learn new habits and to be more transparent and trusting of others. I think that's an adjustment everybody who delivers complex solutions needs to make because it's more aligned with today's owner's challenges.

"For example, our firm is now doing more integrated project delivery work in the construction industry. Because owners realize that they not only have to think about maximizing their initial investment into a new construction project, they also have to make sure it's executed so that it's more operationally efficient over the lifetime the structure is used. Smart owners realize that, by investing time and resources into bringing intelligence into the design process on the front end, they will spend less to build the facility, they will also save money over the long-term through things like better energy efficiency, and lower annual operating costs. This approach feels risky at first because owners are spending more on design than they traditionally do. It's innovative and requires teamwork and collaboration on all fronts – from the owners to all service providers involved in the project. But it pays off."

**MARK D'ARCY**
*SR. HEALTHCARE PROJECT EXECUTIVE AT TURNER CONSTRUCTION COMPANY*
*FORMER VICE PRESIDENT AT BEAUMONT HOSPITAL*

Your P/SDPs will come from an array of industries, both directly related to and outside of the market you're targeting. Together, you will explore each firm's unique capabilities and how you might be able to offer unexpected, dynamic solutions for that market through collaboration with each other. Non-traditional pairings and solutions are what will give you and the organization you lead a competitive edge on the fast-track of innovation.

Don't just say, "I want to work with this company because they look like they would be good to work with." Learn which organizations are good to work with and which would be more difficult by talking with people who have relationships with that organization and why they do. What you learn will help you decide whether or not to work with certain partners.

If you are treating your P/SDP like this...or your partners are treating you like this...then you have a problem:

*Are you part of an opportunist partnership – a one-off partner relationship where work comes in one project at a time? Something happens that prompts you to call them, or them to call you. Maybe they already do business with a mutual customer and you've identified a quick-win opportunity. You only share as much information and client intelligence as you think it demands. And once the project is over or the opportunity dissolves you go your separate ways.*

*Well here's the punch line to that type of relationship...*

*That's not just a single, lost revenue-generating opportunity. It's a lost opportunity for building a different kind of pipeline, a different kind of partnership in which everyone wins.*

*"There is an art and process behind building an effective project delivery team. You have to create alignment and synergy by looking for other individuals and companies who are like-minded, are confident in their abilities and are capable of delivering value in their area of discipline. This is important because, when you share these qualities, you can focus on delivering the right solution for the client. You don't waste time worrying about who is taking the lead and who is controlling the relationship. When people are confident in how they are differentiated and where they're adding value, it builds trust with the other members of the team. Who you put on your project delivery teams is as much about your interpersonal relationships and ability to work together as it is about the skill set.*

*"As you're developing the project delivery partner relationships, you should also be focusing on finding the right owners to do business with. I have sometimes found myself frustrated by the lack of understanding by specific owners on the decision-maker side of the equation because, at times, they don't truly understand what's needed to develop a successful project. Many owners fear that service providers just want to take advantage of them. So when you approach them with a team approach, many owners spend time trying to figure out your angle and how you're going to take advantage of them. Don't spend too much time on owners that won't get it. Cut to the chase pretty quickly because, ultimately, you want an owner that will engage you and see that the team has value and solutions that can help them."*

**WILL HODGES**
**PRESIDENT AT CADENCE MCSHANE CONSTRUCTION COMPANY**

## PATHS TO CONNECTION

In REASSESS, I talked about going to where your clients are going to find the answers. They're going to conferences, reading magazines and business books, listening to podcasts by thought leaders, and following disruptive thinkers on LinkedIn and Twitter. Go where they go, read what they read, listen to the same podcasts. In REFRAME, I gave you some ideas on the better questions you ought to consider asking.

Now it's time to start thinking about how you're physically and socially connected with people in your industry, client and P/SDPs. Did you work with them before? Did one of your friends, employees or business partners work with them before? Are they connected on LinkedIn, Facebook, or Twitter? Did you go to the same school or are you members of the same profes-

RESET

sional organizations? What role do they play in the organization?

## CLIENT ORGANIZATION

- Who is the real decision maker? This is the person who can advance your goals. It isn't always who you would expect. Are you connected (e.g. via your employees, P/SDPs, LinkedIn, Facebook, or alumni association)? How?

- Who are the internal champions? These are the people with leadership-level influence who want you to win for their own "greater good" reasons. Are you connected? How?

- Who are your navigators? These are people who can guide you through the details of the organization. You need at least a couple of navigators. Are you connected? How?

## BUSINESS & POLITICAL ISSUES

- What are the business and political issues that are important for the client to be able to compete more effectively? These are the contextual clues surrounding their challenges and motivations in the marketplace. They are also internal issues floating around in your client's organization.

- What is the order of priority for these issues?

- How are you going to address each of these issues?

- Who, between you and your project delivery partners, can address each of these issues?

## DEMONSTRATING UNDERSTANDING

- Who are the thought leaders in this industry and why? Do you follow them and read their articles, blogs, and e-books?

- What article, conference, or speaker helped you to understand the issue behind the issue?

- Who is going to use this to help position you with which person within the client organization?
- How important is this and when does it need to happen?

A key to developing the path to engagement is empathy. This is how you develop behavioral respect and empathy for your client. Without empathy, you might be considered just another judge-y, know-it-all like the personal trainer Drew Manning was BEFORE he embarked on a career-altering journey:

*[Drew Manning had always been] a fitness junkie, staying in shape comes naturally for Manning. He's that guy at the gym the rest of us love to hate, the one who likes to use his biceps for pumping iron instead of changing channels, and who prefers sucking down a spinach shake to indulging in a brownie sundae.*

*Because of that, Manning was a "judgmental" trainer, his wife says. "He would look at someone who was overweight and say, 'They must really be lazy.'*

*"I was convinced people used genetics or similar excuses as a crutch," Manning writes in his new book, "Fit2Fat2Fit." "You either wanted to be healthy or you didn't."*

*That point of view wasn't helping Manning help his clients. When he failed yet again to push someone over to the light side, he knew something was wrong. In order to better understand the struggles his clients were facing, he had to face them himself.*

*He gave up the gym and started consuming junk food, fast food, and soda. In just six months, he went from 193 pounds with a 34-inch waist to 265 pounds with a 48-inch waist. The fitness trainer's journey had come to an end after successfully losing more than 70 pounds – six months after he purposely gained the same amount.*

*"The biggest thing [I learned] is that it's not just about the physical. It's not just about the meal plan and the workouts and those things. The key is the mental and the emotional issues. I realized those issues are real."*

# CREATE THE PLAYBOOK

I talked about this in REFORM, but it bears repeating. Keep track of all your findings somewhere it can be shared and edited with your P/SDP. You should be able to draw lines of connection between all parts of the information you collect. This cannot be done with traditional CRM software. Again, think of the CSI board. All the pieces of the puzzle are on the board. It's up to you and your P/SDPs and team members to bring your perspectives to bear to see the best possible connections to lead you to the best possible solutions.

*"A disciplined capture-planning process provides sense of purpose and focus to business development activities because it forces you to ask the simple questions, such as:*

1. *Is the client or project worth pursuing?*
2. *What is the overall client structure?*
3. *Who are the influencers? And could they help you hunt down more details about the opportunity?*
4. *Who is also interested in working on this project that you can leverage?*

*"I direct my team to spend a couple of hours doing research and documenting the answers to these basic questions so that we as leadership can make 'go' or 'no-go' decisions. Then if we decide to 'go,' the team layers in more information as it's gathered and we have intentionality behind all of our sales and marketing choices. When done right, the process also gives you common language for*

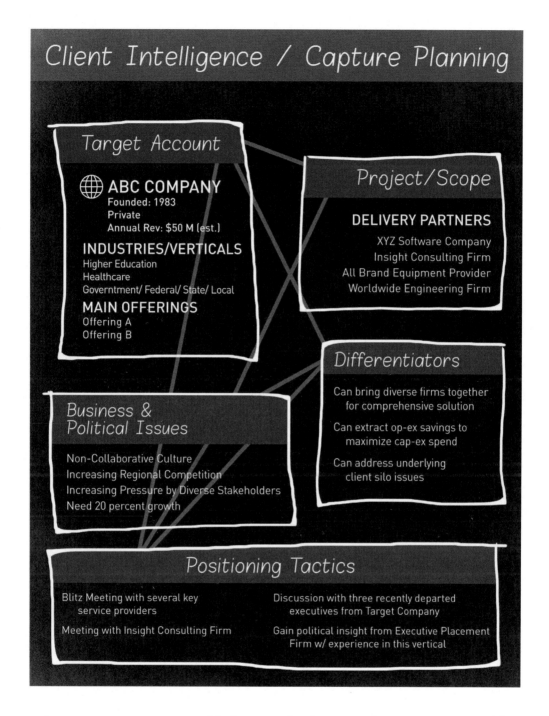

# Client Intelligence / Capture Planning

## Target Account

🌐 **ABC COMPANY**
Founded: 1983
Private
Annual Rev: $50 M (est.)

**INDUSTRIES/VERTICALS**
Higher Education
Healthcare
Governtment/ Federal/ State/ Local

**MAIN OFFERINGS**
Offering A
Offering B

## Project/Scope

**DELIVERY PARTNERS**
XYZ Software Company
Insight Consulting Firm
All Brand Equipment Provider
Worldwide Engineering Firm

## Differentiators

Can bring diverse firms together
for comprehensive solution

Can extract op-ex savings to
maximize cap-ex spend

Can address underlying
client silo issues

## Business & Political Issues

Non-Collaborative Culture
Increasing Regional Competition
Increasing Pressure by Diverse Stakeholders
Need 20 percent growth

## Positioning Tactics

Blitz Meeting with several key
service providers

Meeting with Insight Consulting Firm

Discussion with three recently departed
executives from Target Company

Gain political insight from Executive Placement
Firm w/ experience in this vertical

the entire team to use, and helps everybody get on the same page quickly.

"Collaborative teams selling projects – even across company lines – will
be the way of the future. Competition has gotten more intense, profit
margins are tighter, and the sales costs are going up. The 'everybody in his

RESET

*or her own lane' approach doesn't really work. You have to spread out within your own internal team and outside to your project delivery partners and make everybody a part of the process so that you can all win."*

LEE SLADE
SENIOR PRINCIPAL AT WALTER P MOORE

There are mind-mapping software tools available that will help you draw connections between the different pieces of information you and your partners gather. For example, bubbl.us is an tool that allows maps to be shared between users online.

# GROWING PAINS SIGNAL GROWTH

Are you still wondering why you need to think, question and do things differently? Still wondering why you need to spend so much time and energy getting to know your clients and P/SDPs? You're not alone. As you look at connecting as a collaborative process, different from the food chain, it's going to be clumsy and painful. It's a sign that it's working.

As a culture, we buy into rainmaking and practically idolize the charming, smooth guy with a big rolodex. And doing things this way, doing them differently, feels uncomfortable at best. In my experience, the problem is fear. It could be fear of failure, loss of credibility and dignity, or loss of a job and ego. It could be fear of uncertainty, the untried or the big risk. I see it every day. It's ok to get unnerved because there is no reinforcement of this in our culture, in business. But if you continue doing what you're doing, you're going to continue getting the same results: declining profits, losing your best employees, and calcifying liquidity.

I've spent my considerable career seeing this happen over and over again. And for the last eight years, I've been helping clients – both owners and service providers – find a way to both see and articulate the true value they bring to each other. I have helped company after company survive and grow in down economies and I have shown them how to create sustainable relationships. This is the crux of that entire practice. I don't just preach it – I practice it in my own business.

A normal thing in every session is overwhelming emotional exhaustion. Why do you really need to do this? To gain a measure of peace and influence over the way you grow your practice. What you can't see (but I can from having coached both service providers and leadership) is that you both want the same thing. Remember the Johns Hopkins Orange? You both want different parts of the same orange.

I can almost hear you stating the obvious, "This is a lot of work." You didn't get where you are by being complacent and taking it easy. You just have to work hard in a different way. What you get out of this is more time. (I told you this would be counter-intuitive.) If you take the time upfront to get to know a client, you'll be able to identify the ones you want to work with – as well as those you won't want to work with. How many clients and projects have you wasted time on? "If I'd only known X, I would never have taken on this project/client!"

Armed with your deep knowledge from research, your cadre of stellar delivery partners, and the comprehensive solutions your client didn't know they needed, you get to skip the procurement lane and take the express lane. No more RFPs. That alone should make you sit up and pay attention. So, take the three-to-four months to practice this. Go in through five doors. It's not about winning them all.

While you're sitting up and taking notice, smart potential clients are, too. You keep showing up where they are, asking great questions, and demonstrating your broad and deep understanding of the challenges they face.

*"Paul Erdos, a mathematician, spent a lifetime thinking of problems, working collaboratively to come up with good solutions. He wrote or co-authored 1,475 academic papers, many of them monumental, and all of them substantial. With 485 co-authors, Erdos collaborated with more people than any other mathematician in history. Those lucky 485 are*

*said to have an Erdos number of 1, a coveted code phrase in the mathematics world for having written a paper with the master himself."*

**ERIC BARKER**
**BARKING UP THE WRONG TREE**

Despite his odd behavior and personality quirks, Erdos was a thought leader. He had a passion for finding good problems and working with others to discover solutions. He was a game changer and a prolific solution finder, and he didn't do it alone.[9]

So, as a team, take the time to understand. Stay current. Always. Because the problems, the market, the industry and the laws are always changing – and when that smart client calls you out of the blue, you won't be caught not knowing. More importantly, when you're ready to make your own calls, you'll know exactly who you're calling on and why.

*"Prior to adopting the account development process, we were predominately acquiring work solely through our general contractor relationships. We were not actively identifying potential revenue streams and crafting our own opportunities with owners. We realized that in order to grow, we needed to find a better way to more directly connect with the multiple decision makers within an owner organization.*

*"We also realized that we could not go about this in a cavalier manner. We had to communicate with our current customer base in an appropriate manner so that they understood we were not trying to bypass them. We were simply trying to protect our own business interests and intended to do it in a way that also protected the GC's interests. When you are open about communicating what you're doing to other members of the*

PDP team, you will earn their respect. This is a relationship-based business, so it's critical to carefully think through how you will communicate through every step.

"While the C-Suite does not always want to get into the weeds of choosing sub-contractors for construction projects, they are interested in hearing about solutions that will add value and save them money. As we started to take this more direct route, we did win the work — which was still primarily awarded through our current general contractor relationships. In specific cases, I am 100 percent positive we would not have won the work if we had gone through the traditional channels. We are most effective when we can identify the business and political issues that are vital to our buyers and then develop a focused business case around how our services can help solve those problems."

JONATHAN BLANSCET
P.E.

# RECEIVE

## THE BENEFITS OF
## ALL THIS WORK

*I often refer to the rotating mechanical device called a flywheel that is used to store rotational energy. I want*

*owners and service providers to create flywheels. When you work at building the flywheel, you focus on initi-*

*ating actions that build momentum that continue to work hard long after you've put in the initial effort.*

RESET

# KEEP FEEDING THE CONNECTION FLYWHEEL

At this point, I usually see a combination of *True Grit*-like determination (complete with swagger) and a bit of relief as people realize that, though this is not easy, it IS very doable. Don't be discouraged as you begin to practice all of this and put it into motion. Do you think Michael Jordan got nothing-but-net his first time out on the court?

Once you and your P/SDPs have some practice in, learn to power-through the inertia and start connecting authentically, you will see the flywheel start moving. And once that flywheel gets turning, you will be moving with the energy and vision needed to adapt to the constantly evolving marketplace. Influencing and making thousands of little course corrections as you go is an infinitely easier way to create growth than controlling and trying to stay on track.

Don't confuse the coach with the athlete. The athlete is the star. The coach is there to hold up a mirror to the flaws in your technique and help you fix them.

*"Successful people tend to have a high need for self-determination. In other words, the more leaders commit to coaching and behavioral change because they believe in the value of the process, the more likely the process is to work. The more they feel that the change is being imposed upon them – or that they are just trying it out – the less likely the coaching process is to work."*

**DR. MARSHALL GOLDSMITH**
***WHAT GOT YOU HERE WON'T GET YOU THERE***

You will find a smart client and P/SDPs, and they will be a touchstone to which you can compare potential clients or partners. Your CSI skills for managing all of the client intelligence data collected from your team will sharpen and you will decipher the problem behind the problem more and more quickly. As time goes on, the art of authentic connection will become second nature. Remember that a flywheel also stores energy as it's working. No more wasted energy on RFPs and the proverbial rat race. The better you become at this, the more energy you will be saving for creative professional work and for your personal life.

# REAPING THE REWARDS

Most people associate reaping with harvesting. But the act of reaping is actually cutting so you can gather and store, i.e. harvest, the mature crop.

- When you decide to start looking for the problem behind the problem, you stop selling. You begin to ask different questions, look for better partners, gain insight, and create value.
- When you start engaging and connecting authentically, you stop closing. You start creating work and driving impact.
- When you start leveraging the right service providers, you stop hemorrhaging. You start focusing on the underlying problem and finding solutions that will address multiple issues.
- When you start brutally honest prioritizing, you stop wasting time on the ineffective 80 percent. You start accomplishing the fruitful 20 percent.

This is the true meaning of reaping. And in this context, you're culling and honing old behaviors for better yields.

Of course, the rewards gained are not just about a new way to develop business. The rewards have wider impact. The changes you've made begin a new cycle of both giving and receiving, based on respect, empathy, engagement, and authentic connection. This, in turn, creates a more sustainable, profitable business for you, your clients and your P/SDPs – and that is the long-term, true reward.

In the traditional sales (seduction) model, you compete tooth-and-nail on an RFP that is submitted to someone who is not a decision-maker for the client. You don't have the opportunity to convey your value to the client, and so your only selling point is your price. And the bid falls lower and lower and lower. If you do work with the client, you provide them with a single-serving service and, at the end, they'll say, "Thanks a lot, we'll call you in three years when we need an upgrade." You do this over and over again. When this doesn't work, you hit the corporate happy hour to "drum up new business," buying a big fish drinks with hopes of landing the "big meeting," but when you get the meeting you show up without knowing anything about the client's problems or how to convey your value. The client gets turned off, you can feel that nothing is working and you don't know why, but you continue to follow the RFP and seduction cycle. There is nothing to reap. This is like wandering the scorched earth, searching for nuts and berries.

On the other hand, one of our clients, Assetworks (an asset management company for facilities, real estate, fleet and fuel management and appraisal) elaborates on the importance of good project delivery partners for creating work and authentic connections:

*"As a company, we were not effective in managing partner relationships in the past. Most work came in one at a time in an opportunist-type partnership. Some catalyst would prompt us to discover what a certain company does and we would say, 'We should call them.' We would partner with firms that do business with the same customer. But that client intelligence and partnership was usually short lived after the opportunity went away. What we've learned over the past year of working with WOA is the importance of sharing good relationships with other smart companies that have good relationships and would be smart P/SDPs. While*

*working with Wayne, it was an eye-opener to see how you could work with a partner to leverage client intelligence. Figure out where the smart customers are and where the smart organizations are that you want to go work with instead of just saying that I want to go work with this company because they look like they would be good to work with. You learn a lot more about the account when you talk with people who are already in the door and have relationships. Based on those discussions, you learn which organizations are good to work with and which would be more difficult. That information helps you decide whether or not to work with certain partners."*

**BROC ZAUTNER**
*VICE PRESIDENT OF SALES AND MARKETING AT ASSETWORKS*

## PICTURE A DAY

Your day will start looking more like this:

- Identify a smart client. You are not going to look for the decision maker. You're not setting up a meeting.

- Look for those potential P/SDPs, those service providers who are already working with the client. Ask them how things work, about the staff, the operational model, the competitors.

- Who are the people within the organization who can coach you about what you don't understand or know about the organization (Navigators)?

- Ask yourself how you're going to start the connection process so you don't look like you're just selling.

- Then go back with your diverse team to identify business and political issues.

- Look for internal champion who could have a selfish interest in leveraging the impact of a service provider like you.

- Go down diverse pathways to understand the problems behind the problem.

You must always and consistently try not to sell. Remember, you've reset your thinking and you are now focused on trying to understand how you can connect and engage, not diagnose. You are a *Client Whisperer*. You'll know you're on the right path when you're able to start the discussion by showing that you've done your homework. This may feel risky, but it's calculated, respectful risk-taking.

This will be confusing to most of your clients, so be patient with them. They are unaccustomed to proactivity, creativity, and honesty of intent. The reward is not just the piece of scope. The reward is more often an account that is sustainable, profitable, and professionally satisfying. Owners will feel the difference between being an account versus just a project or a piece of scope. It will resonate with them.

# STAY ON TRACK

In order to reap the rewards of your changes, you need to keep track of everything:

- Your relationships and influence in each segment
- The business and political issues
- The real problems and your solutions

Contact should be irregular and meaningful so clients don't feel like you have them on a schedule. That said, just because it's irregular doesn't mean it's unplanned. You will still need to keep track of when you both contact and plan to contact people, why you're contacting them and what doing so results in.

Everyone on your team needs to do this and stay informed of new developments. Keep track of the progress of both the long and short-term tasks. Regardless of where new information comes from, it needs to reside somewhere that everyone can access. Again, you will need something simpler and more focused on the important leading indicators of revenue generation than traditional CRM software is capable of — something that can track all of the non-linear intelligence that you collect from many diverse sources in order to decipher your client's problem behind the problem. If a new piece of information is a game changer, then be ready to discuss how, who, and what that new information affects and act accordingly. Everyone has to put some skin in the game for this to work. *Everyone* includes you. The harder you and your team work in practice to understand your client, the easier it will be to share an authentic connection when it comes to facilitating decision making for the client. Just like a team training for any sport, practice should always more intense than the actual game. It needs to be so that you and our team are prepared for anything because you've prepared for it during practice. Now that you've learned how to think this way you're relying on the methodology.

# RESPOND

## CONNECT, ENGAGE, SHARE

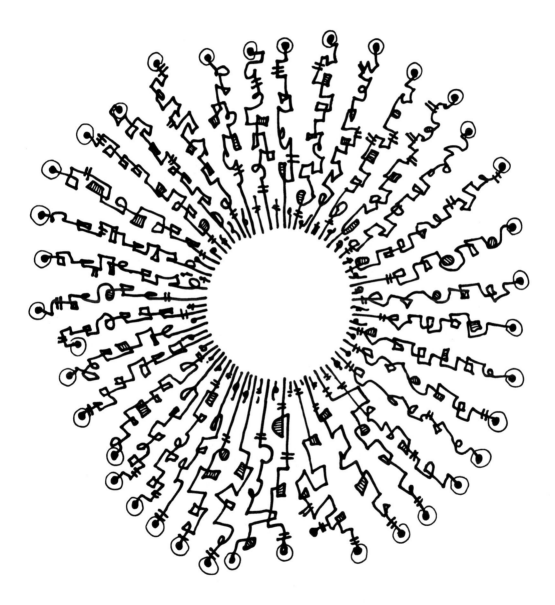

*Your flywheel is full of ideas and connections that extend out, and enable you to respond to your*

*market in repeatable and sustainable ways. And most importantly, you can share these connec-*

*tions within your own ecosystem. Once you figure this out, energy explodes from the center.*

RESET

# HOW ARE YOU GOING TO RESPOND?

Are you ready to build your team? You need to take an active role. You have the power to influence, but you have to slow down to go faster. This is all about the RESET. It will take coaching (not more sales training). It will take mirrors. And it will require this type of thinking and behavior in all levels of your company. And it will take practice before you are ready to navigate the unpredictable waters of today's markets.

*"Traditionally [in the design and construction industry], engineers don't want to usurp the relationships that the architects have with the owners. So in the past they were very cautious to get heavily involved higher up the food chain. Things are different now, and firms are in a position where they have to make a change. For example, structural engineering is highly competitive, and they are not making the level of profitability they are accustomed to making. They are becoming commoditized even though they may be doing high-end commercial work. So they have to find different ways to show value to their clients. They have to become a much more well-rounded consultant and go about building business differently; it's really a part of their emerging leadership skills that they have to develop in their careers.*

*"Building these types of new skills takes a combination of training and coaching. While I have personally built my career around the importance of training to develop leadership skills, I have also seen that there is a powerful combination when you marry coaching with training. Research*

*findings have shown that retention of information and skill building increase tenfold when coaching is provided following training. Also, the best learning experience is when you can squeeze the time between when you learn something new and when you have to put it into practice. Coaching couldn't be a better method for squeezing that gap. It's like learning while you are dealing with live ammunition."*

**LEIGH MIRES**
**CHIEF LEARNING OFFICER, THORNTON TOMASETTI**

You know that you can't do it alone, but only you can empower yourself with the tools and the team to get that flywheel turning. Remember to use social media to your advantage. The world is now connected more than any other time in history. Don't be afraid to reach out to new people or to get reacquainted with older or current contacts.

RESET your perspective on growth and leveraging intellectual talent. The payoff is more rewarding – for your business, your clients, your team members and yourself.

*"When [what you are deeply passionate about, what you can be best in the world at, and what drives your economic engine] come together, not only does your work move toward greatness, but so does your life. For, in the end, it is impossible to have a great life unless it is a meaningful life. And it is very difficult to have a meaningful life without meaningful work. Perhaps, then, you might gain that rare tranquility that comes from knowing that you've had a hand in creating something of intrinsic excellence that makes a contribution. Indeed, you might even gain that deepest of all satisfactions: knowing that your short time here on this earth has been well spent, and that it mattered."*

**JIM COLLINS**
**GOOD TO GREAT: WHY SOME COMPANIES MAKE THE LEAP ... AND OTHERS DON'T**

# WHAT I WANT YOU TO BUY IS...
# STOP SELLING

What I just gave you is a roadmap for connecting to grow your business. To help you crystallize

your thoughts and provide some structure, here is an image that represents the methodology:

*Stop selling. Start connecting.*

# WHERE TO FIND MORE

By all means, contact me – I always respond. I'll even make it easy for you by providing

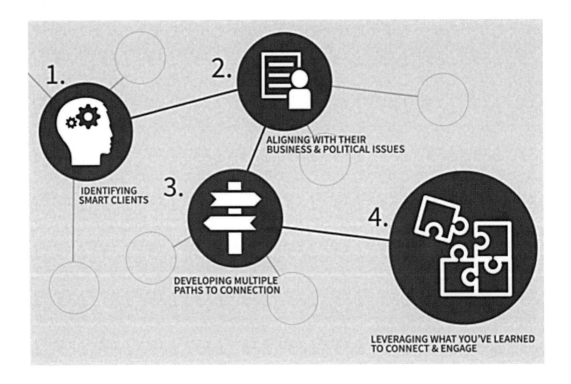

you a list of how to reach me via social media below. And do read my blog (woassociates.com); you may very well find the answer you're looking for there.

**Blog:** woassociates.com/blog

**LinkedIn:** linkedin.com/in/wayneoneill

**Twitter:** @woassociates

# REFERENCE

1.      Malcolm Gladwell, *Outliers: The Story of Success* (New York: Little, Brown & Co; 2008)

2.      Miller GA (March 1956). "The magical number seven plus or minus two: some limits on our capacity for processing information". Psychological Review 63 (2): 81–97. Republished: Miller GA (April 1994). "The magical number seven, plus or minus two: some limits on our capacity for processing information. 1956". Psychological Review 101 (2): 343–52.

3.      Brian Halligan, "Inbound Marketing vs. Outbound Marketing," HubSpot, available at http://blog.hubspot.com/blog/tabid/6307/bid/2989/Inbound-Marketing-vs-Outbound-Marketing.aspx

4.      Encyclopedia Brittanica definition of Flywheel, available at http://www.britannica.com/EBchecked/topic/211745/flywheel

5.      Michael Lewis, *Moneyball: The Art of Winning an Unfair Game* (New York: W.W. Norton & Company, Inc.; 2004)

6.      David Kelley, "Design Thinking," Fast Company Magazine

7.      Doug Lemov, Erica Woolway and Katie Yezzi, *Practice Perfect: 42 Rules for Getting Better at Getting Better* (San Francisco: Jossey-Bass; 2012)

8.      Jacque Wilson, "Fitness trainer gains and loses 70 pounds in 1 year – on purpose," CNN Health, available at http://www.cnn.com/2012/06/05/health/drew-manning-fit2fat2fit-lessons/index.html

9.      Eric Barker, "Erdos: 3 Key Life Lessons You Can Learn From A Very Odd Mathematician," Barking up the Wrong Tree, available at http://www.bakadesuyo.com/2013/07/erdos/#ixzz2bC2wsrkD

36677619R00052

Made in the USA
Middletown, DE
07 November 2016